PRIVATE LESSONS

by
Ed Roscetti

Also by Ed Roscetti:

Drummer's Guide to Odd Meters....00695349
Blues Drumming..............................00695623

You can correspond with Ed Roscetti at:
bpmrecords@earthlink.net

or visit his website at
www.roscettimusic.com
and
www.worldbeatrhythms.com

ISBN 0-634-03874-5

HAL•LEONARD®
CORPORATION
7777 W. BLUEMOUND RD. P.O. BOX 13819 MILWAUKEE, WI 53213

Copyright © 2003 by HAL LEONARD CORPORATION
International Copyright Secured   All Rights Reserved

No part of this publication may be reproduced in any form
or by any means without the prior written permission of the Publisher.

Visit Hal Leonard Online at
www.halleonard.com

About the Author

Originally from Niagara Falls, New York, **ED ROSCETTI** is a drummer, composer, and educator now living and working in Los Angeles. He is a contributing author for *Modern Drummer magazine* and a curriculum author at Musicians Institute (PIT). He is also co-founder and co-author of the "World Beat Rhythms" workshop series and soon-to-be released book/CD series. His critically praised *Drummer's Guide to Odd Meters* (published by Hal Leonard Corporation) was chosen as the number two method book in *Drum Magazine's* 2001 readers poll, and his most recently released book/CD is *Blues Drumming*.

Ed has worked or collaborated with the likes of Quincy Jones, Herbie Hancock, Joe Sample, the Crusaders, Barry Mann/Cynthia Weil, Benny Golson, Robben Ford, Jeff Baxter, Tommy Tedesco, Joe Porcaro, and Jeff Porcaro, among others. His composing and arranging credits include "Saturday Night Live," "General Hospital," "Santa Barbara," "Knight Rider," "Sunset Beach," "Lifestyles of the Rich and Famous," and movies of the week *The 60's* and *The Secret.* He is also an active songwriter and record producer.

Professional Affiliations: American Society of Composers, Authors, and Publishers (ASCAP), National Association of Recording Arts and Sciences (NARAS), American Federation of Musicians (AFM), and the Society of Composers and Lyricists (SCL)

Credits

Drums and Percussion: Ed Roscetti
Keyboards: Ed Roscetti
Guitars: Pathik Desai
Bass: Ed Roscetti, Silvio Bruno
Additional Keyboards: Silvio Bruno

DAW Tech: John Hartmann
CD Mastering: Damon Tedesco
Drum Tech/Cartage: Tim Metz
Studio Tech: Dean Alling

All songs composed, arranged, and produced by Ed Roscetti, Groovetoons (ASCAP) © 2002. Recorded and mixed at Groovetoons and BPM Productions, Studio City, California by Ed Roscetti and Silvio Bruno.

Special thanks to: Claudia Dunn, Maria Martinez, John Hartmann, Pathik Desai, Joe Porcaro, John Snider, Curt Bisquera, Damon Tedesco, Tim Metz, Dean Alling, Louie Marino, my loving partner Claudia and my family Armeto, Ann, and Linda Roscetti, Groovetoons, BPM Productions, World Beat Rhythms, and everyone at Hal Leonard Corporation.

Thank you for your support: Scott Donnell (Drum Workshop/Pacific); Rich Mangicaro (Paiste); Carol Calato and Dan Schieder (Regal Tip); Gavin Carignan, Bill Carson, and Brock Kaericher (Remo); Terry Bissette and Lionel Barton (Sam Ash); Ryan Smith (Shure, Inc.); Michael Marans (Event Electronics); Chrissy Laughlin (Emagic); Su Littlefield, Chandra Lynn, and Danielle Parker (DigiDesign); Rick Naqvi (PreSonus); Ryan (Mountain Rhythms)

Ed Roscetti uses the following equipment and software: Pacific LX series drumset (Drum Workshop/Pacfic); Paiste cymbals (Paiste); Remo drum heads and world percussion (Remo); sticks, brushes, and mallets (Regal Tip); KSM 32's, KSM 27's, and Beta series microphones (Shure, Inc.); 20/20 biamplified studio monitors and 5.1 Surround (Event Electronics); Protools LE (001) (DigiDesign); Unitor II MK and E-Logic Platinum software (Emagic); Digimax Mic Pre (PreSonus)

This book is dedicated to my friend John Snider, who grooves hard and always has a smile on his face.

Contents

Foreword

With this book/CD, Ed Roscetti has combined all of his experience and knowledge as a drummer, producer, composer, and educator to bring you a funk and hip-hop learning experience that has the pulse of the street and a strong connection to the technology-driven music business of today.

Ed's playing, programming, and loop concepts are a must in building your rhythmic and groove vocabulary—utilizing kick, snare, and hi-hat combinations, fills, and phrasing ideas to fortify your styles. This book is your bread and butter!

—*Joe Porcaro*

Introduction

In these contemporary times, I often ask myself, "Where have all the people gone?" Computers, software, hard discs, plug-ins, keyboards, monitors, mice… Sometimes it seems like, if we let it happen, technology will take over completely. (Hey, sounds like my studio!)

In my own career, I've seen things come full circle—from my beginnings as a teenager playing in garage bands and at high school dances, moving to L.A. in the late '70s and recording in sessions, through my drum-programming, composing, and producing years of the '80s, into drum loops of the '90s and back to real drums in the new millenium. To the modern drummer working today, the mixing and combination of real live drums, programmed beats, and overdubs is essential. It all comes down to the piece of music or song and how it affects you. Whether there are drums or not, a great piece of music is a great piece of music.

You've probably experienced that a lot of the drumbeats today are programmed or are drum loops. Just listen to the music, and concentrate on playing along, developing a good, strong feel within your grooves. Get into programming your own beats and making your own loops. Use all the new technology to help you create your music. In the music business of today, styles are being melded together more than ever. Keep your eyes and ears open. Be it a live drummer, a programmed groove, a drum loop, or a combination of all three, if a great song and a great groove are the end result, that's all that matters.

I hope this book/CD helps you improve your time feel and expand your musicality in the funk and hip-hop genre.

Ed Roscetti

You can correspond with Ed Roscetti at: *bpmrecords @earthlink.net* or visit his website at *www.roscettimusic.com* and *www.worldbeatrhythms.com*.

How to Use This Book

Funk and Hip-Hop Drumming is set up as a workbook. The more grooves, fills, and phrasing ideas that you write and perform with the CD, the more progress you'll make in the style. Each chapter features a different funk/hip-hop song for you to play along with. To help you navigate each song, you'll find the following in every chapter:

Grooves: One-, two-, and four-bar grooves that work with the song. These will help you with the basic time feel and get you started playing.

Fills & Phrasing: Two-beat, three-beat, or other-length fill ideas for "filling in" at the end of phrases and sections. This includes ideas for "ensemble phrases."

Chart: The form of the song—Intro, A section, B section, etc. Chords symbols are included.

At the start of each chapter, listen to the CD to get a feel for the song. Then begin working on the grooves, fills, and phrases shown. (Be sure to write your own, too, on the worksheets provided!) Then, when you're ready, play along with the chart at the end of the chapter.

Although you can jump around the chapters, it's best to work on them in order. In addition to listening to and playing along with the CD tracks, I recommend getting together with other musicians—especially a bass player—to play these charts, using different grooves and tempos. This will help you develop your internal clock and time feel away from the CD.

Also, don't forget to spend time listening to various funk and hip-hop artists while you're working on the grooves in this book.

Good luck, and have fun!

About the CD

On the accompanying CD, you'll hear each chart played twice: first with drums, and then again without. On the tracks with drums, the concentration is on demonstrating the time feel. On the tracks without, the purpose is to play along. The "play-along" backing tracks have a one-bar count-off (four hi-hat clicks) before the downbeat. A cowbell click or hi-hat keeps time through the remainder of the song. Use the grooves and fills in this book—as well as your own grooves and fills—when playing along with these tracks.

Notation Key

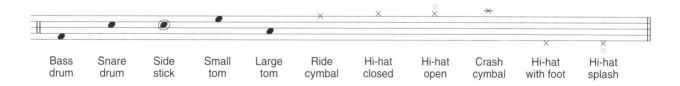

| Bass drum | Snare drum | Side stick | Small tom | Large tom | Ride cymbal | Hi-hat closed | Hi-hat open | Crash cymbal | Hi-hat with foot | Hi-hat splash |

The Funk and Hip-Hop Style

Regardless of the style you choose to play, playing drums is not just about playing in time; it's about playing with the right *time feel.* You get the attitude, vibe, and feeling from the songs and by listening to other musicians play. Listen and saturate yourself in the style that you want to play. Feel the music, and play along with CDs. Remember: you can't get everything from a book; you need to find the groove within yourself. It's not always what you play, but how you play it.

Here's a quick rundown of some artists to check out in the funk and hip-hop style.

Funk

The word *funk* originated from a slang term for "stink." Funk was the rawest form of R&B music. It was less structured than traditional R&B, and the song forms expanded into extended jam sessions of Africanized rhythms built on subdivided and syncopated grooves. Funk originally appealed only to the hardcore R&B audiences.

The most important aspect of funk music was, and is, the groove. The band members move and play off of one another to create a time feel that is of one entity (for example, "All in All" by Earth, Wind & Fire). The music uses low-end ostinato bass lines, two to three rhythm guitarists playing single-note lines and riffs together, and a drum groove with a deep, syncopated pocket.

Funk allowed for more freedom and improvisation within the song form than R&B did. It was similar to what was going on around the same time in blues-rock, psychedelia, and hard rock. (Jimi Hendrix was a huge inspiration for funk guitar soloists.) In soul hits "Papa's Got a Brand New Bag" (1965) and "Cold Sweat" (1967) by James Brown, you can hear the roots of funk rhythms emerge. Sly and the Family Stone was influenced by soul, psychedelia, and rock, leaning into funk with the 1969 hit "Stand." But the official funk anthem was James Brown's 1970 "Get Up (I Feel Like Being a) Sex Machine." George Clinton's Parliament and Funkadelic Ensemble turned funk into the ultimate party music, with musicians, singers, and dancers on stage doing long, extended jams. When disco came into the picture in the mid '70s, funk became smoother and lost some of its original earthiness.

Funk has had a major influence on jazz. Listen to Miles Davis's *The Man with a Horn* and *Tuttu.* It has also become a main musical influence of hip-hop. Funk enjoyed a return in the '90s among white audiences who wanted to explore the original classics. Listen to the following artists, and you will find the drummers that you need to listen to.

Suggested Artists:

Isaac Hayes	Herbie Hancock	Chic
Prince	Curtis Mayfield	Earth, Wind & Fire
The Ohio Players	Miles Davis	Rick James
Tower of Power	Stevie Wonder	Sly and the Family Stone
Chaka Khan	Brecker Bros.	George Clinton
The Average White Band	The Brothers Johnson	Michael Jackson
Rufus	The Time	The Jacksons
The Isley Brothers	James Brown	

Hip-Hop

The term *hip-hop* comes from a lifestyle referring to culture, graffiti, break dancing, and rapping, with turntable scratching surrounding the music. Stylistically, hip-hop refers to music created with those elements in mind.

Hip-hop is the culture from which rap emerged. Once rap had been established and had history, hip-hop looked back to the old regime of artists—including MCs like Kurtis Blow and Whodini and DJs like Grand Master Flash and Afrika Bambaataa. Hip-hop has its own language, style of dress, music, and state of mind that is constantly changing.

Suggested Artists:

Afrika Bambaataa	Beastie Boys	Coolio
Ice Cube	Dr. Dre	Queen Latifah
Will Smith	DMX	Eminem
LL Cool J	Kurtis Blow	Timbaland

G-Funk

G-funk is the lazy, behind-the-beat, Parliament/Funkadelic-influenced variation of gangsta rap created by Dr. Dre in the early '90s. With its low-end bass grooves, synths, slow-grooving programmed drumbeats, and generic female backup vocals, G-funk became the most popular genre of hip-hop in the early '90s. With the success of his 1992 album *The Chronic*—in which he invented and named the style—Dr. Dre opened the door and influenced many new rap artists and producers who used his musical techniques to make a recognizable sound in rap for most of the early '90s.

Listen to the rhythms and the rhymes of the raps and the programmed drum and bass grooves.

Suggested Artists:

Dr. Dre: *2001* (1999)
Snoop Doggy Dogg: *Last Meal* (2000), *Dogg Father* (1996)
2 Pac: *Me Against the World* (1995)
Ice Cube: *Predator* (1992)

The music on the play-along CD is a hybrid of some of the funk and hip-hop styles that have influenced me over the years. Have fun playing the charts.

Chapter One

FEELING THE DOWNBEATS

Developing a strong and consistent backbeat is very important when playing funk grooves. In this chapter, we'll concentrate on feeling the downbeats (1, 2, 3, and 4) on the hi-hat or ride while playing straight backbeats (2 and 4) on the snare.

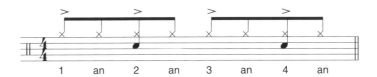

A sense of forward motion is created in our time feel when we emphasize the downbeats (accent the quarter notes) on the hi-hat or ride.

Listen to CD Track 1 to hear the time feel, and follow along with Chart 1, CD Track 1 "Medium Funk," at the end of this chapter. Then start working on the following grooves, fills, and phrases.

Grooves

Let's begin with some one-bar grooves that will work in the Intro and Section A of our song. For these grooves, be sure to emphasize the backbeats on the snare (on 2 and 4), indicated with accents. The unaccented snare hits should be played softly —as ghost notes.

For these and all the grooves in this book, try this practice approach:

- First, set your metronome or drum machine to the CD tempo (♩=96) and start working on the grooves, one at a time—until you feel you've mastered them. (This may take a while.)
- Next, work them within the metronome range suggested (♩=76-106). Get comfortable playing each individual groove at different tempos.
- Then, play each groove two times each, one leading into the next.
- Also try jumping around the page, playing one into the next as two-bar phrases.
- Play with dynamics: soft (*p*), medium (*mf*), and loud (*f*).

Only count at first if you have to. As soon as you can, stop counting. Use your ears, and play by feel. *Let's groove!*

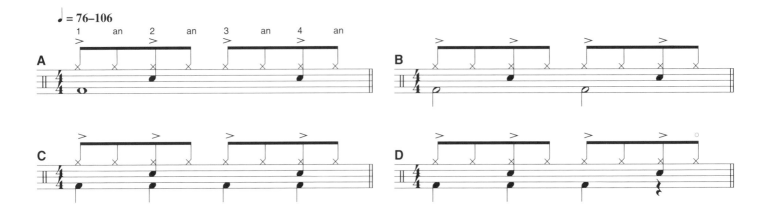

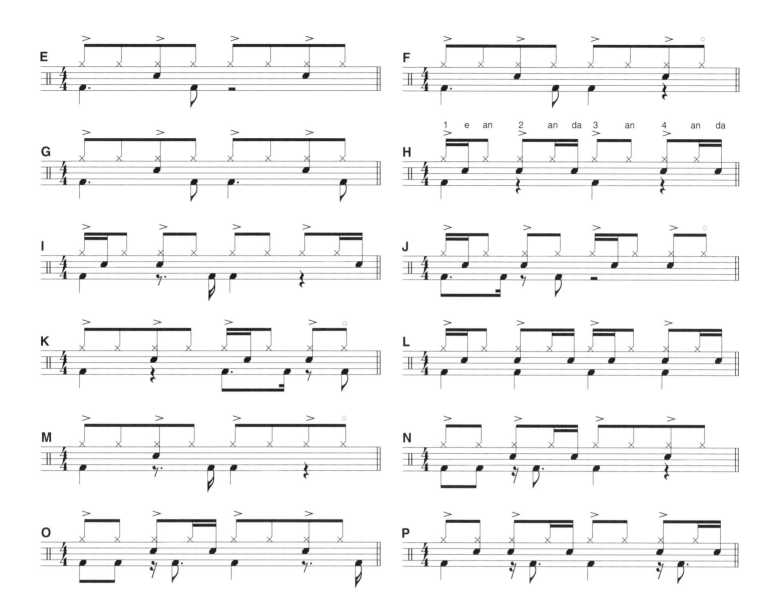

The following two-bar grooves will work with Section B. These are more syncopated than the Section A grooves. Work them the same way. Accented snare hits should be played loudly. Stay relaxed, and be sure not to grip your sticks too tightly. Let the groove breathe.

Worksheet

As you're working on these grooves (and the following fills), create some of your own using this worksheet. Include metronome markings, and keep your examples organized.

Fills & Phrasing

Now it's time to check out some orchestrated fill ideas. The following fills each occupy two beats of time feel. Pick a previous groove and play two beats of it into one of these two-beat fills over and over again until it feels comfortable and relaxed. Then, experiment with different combinations.

two-bar phrase = 1 1/2 bars of groove plus fill

four-bar phrase = 3 1/2 bars of groove plus fill

Before we play Chart 1, let's also check out the ensemble figure that appears at the end of Section A. This is played by guitar. I'll subdivide the sixteenth notes so you can easily see the syncopation.

How you handle this passage as a drummer is really up to you. You could choose to play *with* it, or around it. The following is a four-bar phrase with the ensemble figure in the fourth measure. Repeat it at different tempos until it's smooth. Also try your own ideas, and listen to the CD.

CHART 1
Medium Funk

TRACK 1   TRACK 2
with drums   without drums

Time to play the whole song. Listen to Track 1 to refresh your memory on the time feel and song form, then play along with Track 2. Use the previous grooves, fills, and phrases to play along. Then try your own grooves and fills. Let's begin.

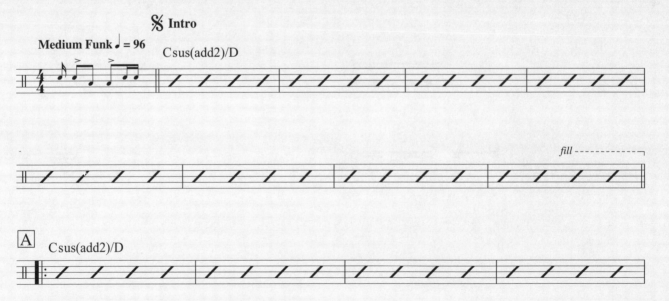

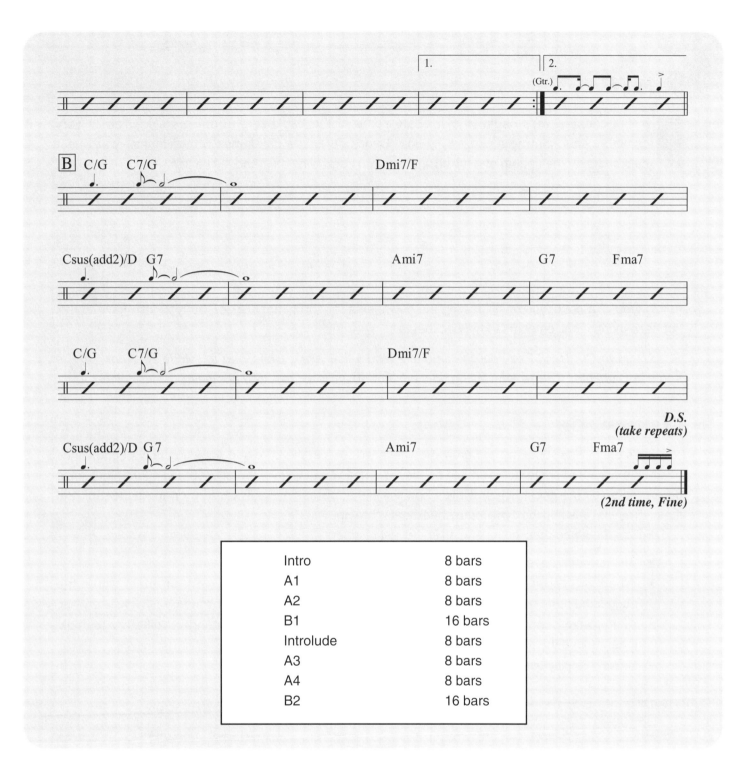

Intro	8 bars
A1	8 bars
A2	8 bars
B1	16 bars
Introlude	8 bars
A3	8 bars
A4	8 bars
B2	16 bars

Chapter Two

SYNCOPATED BACKBEATS

n this chapter, we'll begin to syncopate some of the backbeats in our grooves. This is very common when playing funk and hip-hop. Check out some old James Brown tunes—you'll hear backbeats on the upbeat of 4 mixed with straight backbeats on 2 and 4, like this:

In this type of groove, you're still feeling the downbeats (on the hi-hat or ride), but you also have to feel upbeat syncopations on some of the backbeats.

Listen to CD Track 3 to hear the time feel, and follow along with Chart 2, "Moderate Funk," at the end of this chapter. Then start working on the following grooves, fills, and phrases.

Grooves

Let's begin with some two-bar grooves. These will work in the Intro and A section of our song. Once again, the accented snare notes should be played as backbeats, while the unaccented snare hits should be played softly (as ghost notes). Notice how the hi-hat occasionally disappears on the upbeat of 4 in these grooves; this lets the syncopated backbeats "breathe."

Follow the same practice routine as in the last chapter:

- Set your metronome or drum machine to the CD tempo (♩=120 bpm).
- When you've mastered the grooves at that tempo, go back and work on them within the suggested metronome range (♩=110-130). Go up or down one bpm at a time.
- After you're comfortable playing each two-bar groove (without counting) at different tempos, jump around the page, playing one into the next.
- Be sure to play with dynamics.

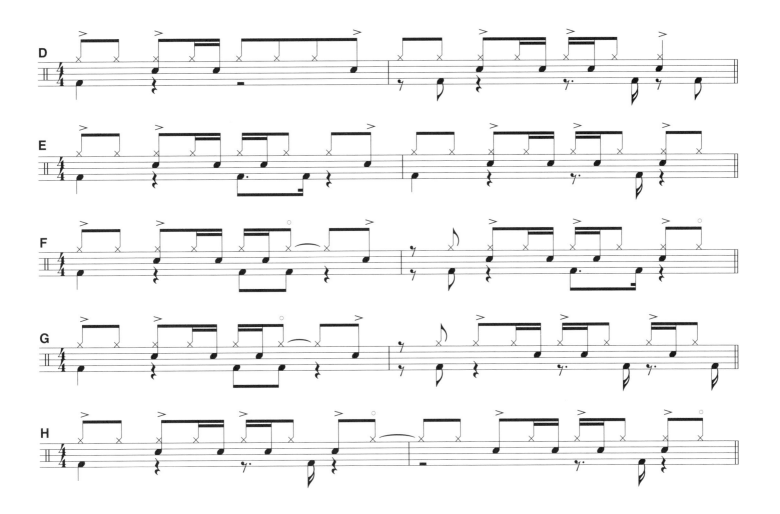

At the end of Section A, there's a turnaround leading back into the intro/breakdown. This later becomes a tag. Listen to the clavinet part. In the third bar, it plays sixteenth notes subdivided into groups of twos and threes. The twos and threes make four groupings of fives to go over the bar line and then resolve on beat 2 of the fourth bar.

As a drummer, you can handle this any number of ways. Begin by playing Example A, the four-bar phrase on the snare drum with quarter notes on the bass drum. This will help you feel the rhythm. Then try Example B, the same idea played as a groove with a fill. Remember to stay relaxed, and groove. Try your own ideas once you're comfortable with this.

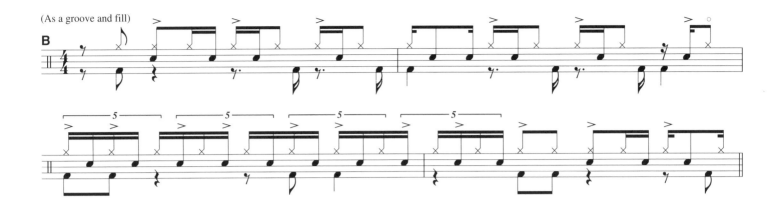

Worksheet

After you have mastered these grooves (and fills), create some of your own on this worksheet.

Fills & Phrasing

Let's begin by playing some two-beat fill ideas. Pick any previous groove and play it into one of the following two-beat fills (A-H) over and over again until the time feel is relaxed. Make sure the fill comes from the time feel of the groove; this will ensure that it sounds like they belong together. Also, be sure to experiment with different phrase combinations:

one-bar phrase = 2 beats of groove plus fill

two-bar phrase = 1 1/2 bars of groove plus fill

four-bar phrase = 3 1/2 bars of groove plus fill

Repeat the same procedure with the three-beat fills (I-P). Use dynamics, work on different tempos, and follow the metronome markings.

CHART 2
Moderate Funk

TRACK 3
with drums

TRACK 4
without drums

It's now time to play along with the CD. Remember to use the grooves and fills in the book first, and then experiment with some of your own. Let's groove. (Listen to Track 3 to hear the drums; then play along with Track 4.)

FYI: Check out the programmed drums in the Intro. You may want to play less during this section.

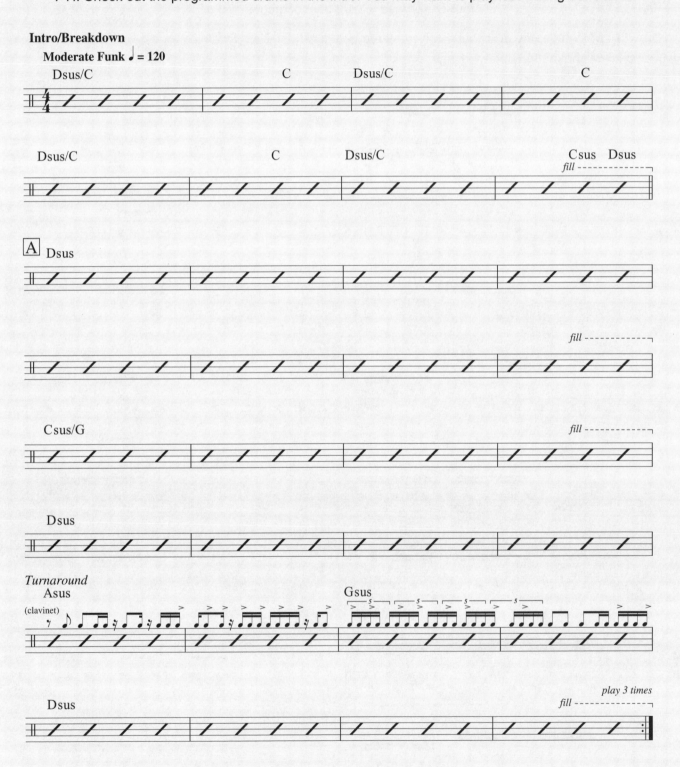

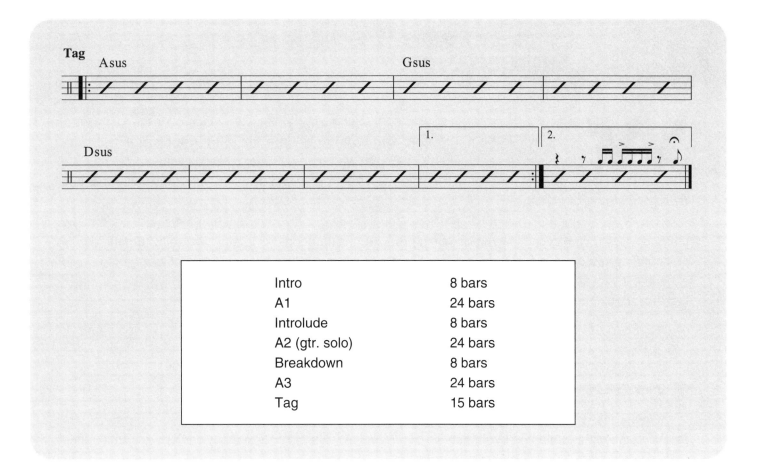

Intro	8 bars
A1	24 bars
Introlude	8 bars
A2 (gtr. solo)	24 bars
Breakdown	8 bars
A3	24 bars
Tag	15 bars

Chapter Three
3
IN BETWEEN STRAIGHT AND SWING

With all the drum programming and sequencing that's taken place over the last twenty years, we've begun to hear some different time feels. In order to relate to the programmed beats and grooves that we hear, we must make adjustments in how we play. Sometimes the groove is somewhere in the middle of straight and swing time—this is called *different increments of swing*.

There is no right or wrong in this process. You just have to find the spot that feels good, and make the song feel right. If you were programming grooves using sequencing software (e.g., Emagic Logic Platinum), you'd be able to select your quantization and your different increments of swing; you could experiment with the groove or loop until it felt right in the track. We must do this when we play as well—find that spot in the time feel that makes the track happen.

Listen to CD Track 5 to hear the time feel, and follow along with Chart 3, "Hip-Hop," at the end of this chapter. Then start working on the following grooves, fills, and phrases.

Grooves

These one-bar grooves will work in the Intro and A Section of the chart. In these grooves, you're bouncing the eighth notes on the hi-hat. Do not accent downbeats or upbeats. Just let the stick bounce and create a nice forward loping sound on the hi-hat. The accents written in the following one-bar grooves are for the snare drum backbeat only—do not accent the hi-hat on 2 and 4. Let's groove!

- First work on the grooves at the CD tempo (♩=86).
- Next, go back and work them within the suggested metronome range (♩=76-96).
- Once you're comfortable with the grooves individually, jump around the page, playing one example into the next. You can also play three bars of one example into one bar of another to make a four-bar phrase. Mix it up and have fun with it.
- Remember to play with dynamics: soft soft (*p*), medium (*mf*), and loud (*f*).

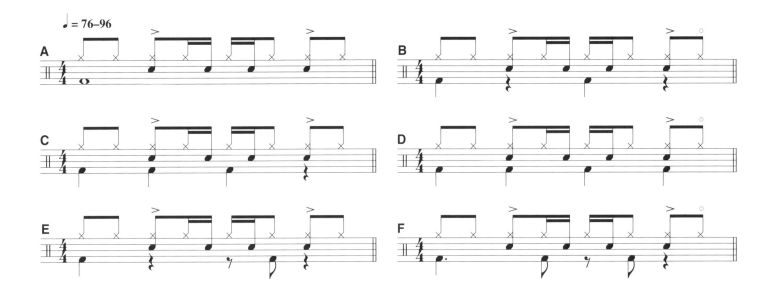

The following two-bar grooves work well with Section B. These grooves are more open than the Section A grooves. Section B has a more "quarter-note" feel in the hi-hat. Work these grooves using the same methods discussed.

Worksheet

After you've worked on grooves for Sections A and B, write some of your own on this worksheet. Always work within the metronome markings.

Fills & Phrasing

We're now going to subdivide sixteenth notes into groups of twos, threes, and ones to create different syncopations and longer fill ideas.

Work on the snare drum examples first (A-H). After you get a good feel playing the rhythms on snare, start orchestrating them on the drumset. The fills shown (I-P) will get you started. Practice each fill by itself, and then in conjunction with a groove: play three bars of a groove and one bar of a fill. This will give you a four-bar phrase. Experiment with different combinations. Remember to make the fill come from the time feel of the groove.

Before we play the chart, let's look at the ensemble figures that set up Section B and close it out. The first one is eighth-note offbeats. The second is quarter-note downbeats.

Work on going from the groove into each figure and then back into the groove again. Continue to play at different tempos, and use dynamics.

CHART 3
Hip-Hop

TRACK 5
with drums

TRACK 6
without drums

Now you're ready to play the song. Listen to Track 5 to refresh your memory on the time feel and song form, then play along with Track 6. Use the previous grooves and fill ideas first. Then experiment with your own grooves and fills. Let's begin.

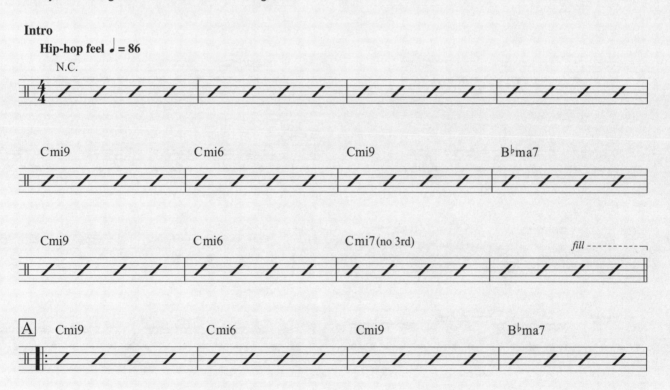

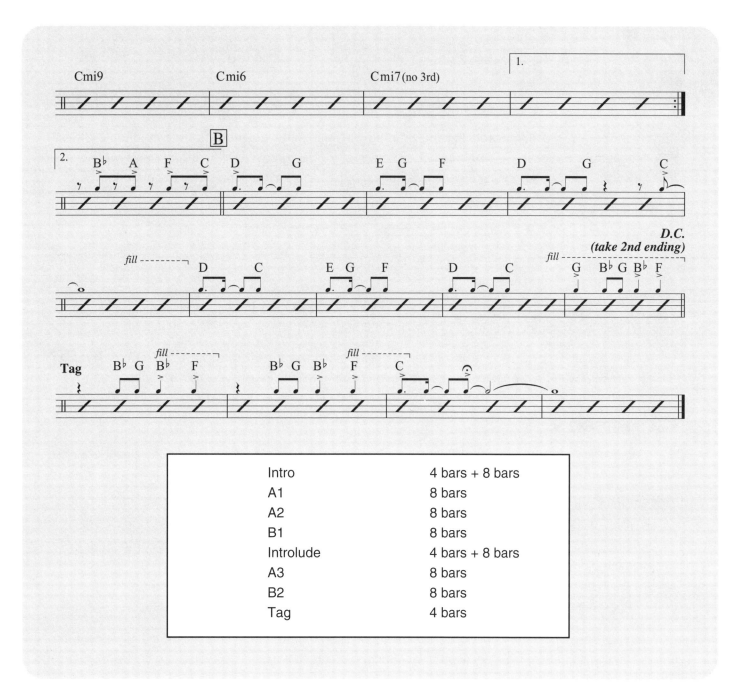

Intro	4 bars + 8 bars
A1	8 bars
A2	8 bars
B1	8 bars
Introlude	4 bars + 8 bars
A3	8 bars
B2	8 bars
Tag	4 bars

Chapter Four

4 FEELING THE UPBEATS

n Chapter 1, we discussed the importance of feeling the downbeats. In this chapter, we'll concentrate on feeling the upbeats. The time feel for our grooves, fills, and phrases will have a forward motion accent of the eighth-note upbeats (the "an's") in the lope of the hi-hat or ride.

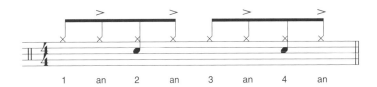

As in the previous chapter, the time feel is swing, but not swung 100%.

Listen to CD Track 7 to hear the time feel, and follow along with Chart 4, CD Track 7 "Hip-Hop Swing," at the end of this chapter. Then start working on the following grooves, fills, and phrases.

Grooves

These one-bar grooves work with the Intro and Section A of our song. Follow the usual practice routine:

- First work the grooves at the CD tempo (♩=106).
- Next, work them within the suggested metronome range (♩=86-120).
- Once you're comfortable playing them individually (without counting) at different tempos, play each groove two times each, one leading into the next.
- Try jumping around the page, playing one groove into the next as two-bar phrases.
- Play with dynamics: soft (*p*), medium (*mf*), and loud (*f*).

NOTE: The accents (>) above the backbeats on 2 and 4 are for the snare only; do not accent the hi-hat. Unaccented snare hits should be played softly—as ghost notes.

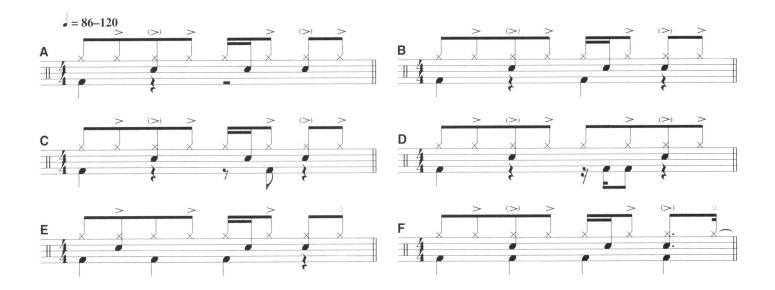

26

The following two-bar grooves work with Section B. They have more syncopation in the hi-hat than the Section A grooves. Play the hi-hat line on the ride cymbal as well. Stay relaxed, and don't grip the sticks too tight.

Worksheet

Be sure to write some of your own grooves (and fills) on this worksheet.

Fills & Phrasing

Let's play some fills with a swing hip-hop feel. Play these coming from any of the previous grooves. Work on them using a four-bar phrase: three bars of time feel and then the fill bar. Experiment with different combinations as in the previous chapters. Keep in mind that repetition is the key to bringing a new idea into your time feel.

Before we play the chart, let's check out the ensemble figure that appears at the end of Section A, setting up Section B. I subdivided the sixteenth notes so you can easily see the syncopation.

Try this four-bar phrase with the ensemble figure in the fourth bar. Repeat it until it's smooth at different tempos. When you have it together, work out some phrases of your own.

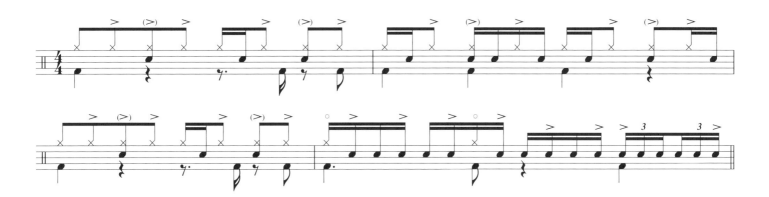

CHART 4
Hip-Hop Swing

TRACK 7 with drums   TRACK 8 without drums

Time to put it all together. Listen to Track 7 for the time feel, then play along with Track 8. Use the grooves, fills, and phrases in the text, and then play your own. Let's begin.

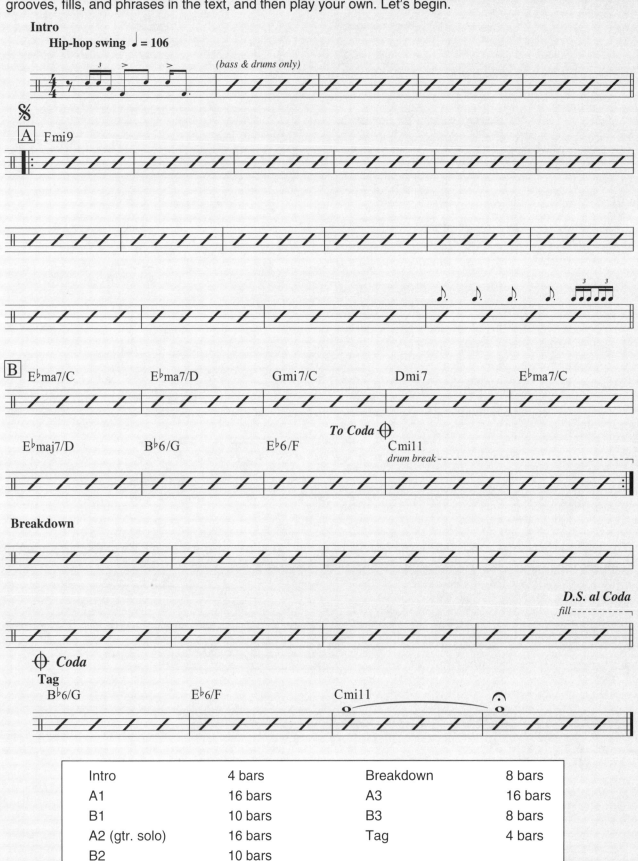

Intro	4 bars	Breakdown	8 bars
A1	16 bars	A3	16 bars
B1	10 bars	B3	8 bars
A2 (gtr. solo)	16 bars	Tag	4 bars
B2	10 bars		

Three Ways to Explore and Play Time

I am now going to discuss three ways to work on your time and time feel: 1) develop your internal clock, 2) play with clicks, and 3) play with drum machines, sequencers, and loops. I strongly suggest you go back and review the grooves, fills, and phrases in the previous chapters utilizing these three concepts.

#1: Develop Your Internal Clock

The first way to work on your time feel is to develop your human clock or internal clock. Count yourself in and play a groove at any tempo for 3-5 minutes. Record yourself with a tape recorder and listen back. See how steady the time was from beginning to end. Do the same procedure when you are rehearsing or on a gig with your band. This will make you aware of your internal clock. Ask yourself: Am I rushing, slowing down, or am I in the pocket? Is the bass player pushing or dragging the time?

The stronger your inner clock is, the more people will want to lean on your time feel and groove with you. Keep in mind that your internal clock is not a drum machine. It does not have perfect time. When you're playing with your internal clock, the time feel should breathe. Work on all your grooves, fills, and phrasing ideas at different tempos and develop a strong internal clock.

#2: Play with a Click

The second way to work on your time feel is with a click. When I play with a click, I like it to be a cowbell playing quarter notes. This way, I pretend I'm playing with a percussionist who is laying down quarter notes. If you relax and are grooving in the middle of the time, you can almost cancel out the click. Remember that the click is only a guide, and it is not part of the track. If the band rushed the click slightly on the outro of the song, you could still keep the take in the studio if the vibe was happening and everyone moved slightly together. Work on playing with different clicks at different tempos. Try to record yourself with a click, and listen back to see where you're putting the time feel in relation to the click.

#3: Play with Drum Machines, Sequencers, and Loops

The third way to work on your time feel is with a drum machine, loops, or sequenced tracks. With a drum machine, loop, or sequenced track, your time feel needs to be more "straight up and down" and fit into the part. This will be the tightest time feel you have to play. Work on programming percussion beds that you can play along to. Also programming synth bass and other rhythm section instruments to play with will help you with this kind of time feel. Playing to CDs that use sequenced tracks and loops is also a big help. That will also help you with your song form development.

Chapter Five
5 HIP-HOP SHUFFLE

n this chapter, we're going to work on a funky hip-hop shuffle. You need to feel the sixteenth-note triplets over this time feel even though sometimes you don't play the triplets. Check out this rhythm exercise to get a feel for the groove.

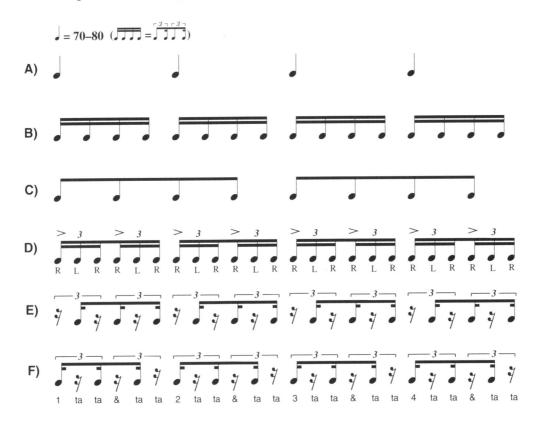

Play example A in your feet (quarter notes in the bass drum or hi-hat) while you play examples B-F in your hands. Play examples B-F over and over.

- Follow the bpm range: ♩=70-80. Start at a slow tempo (e.g., ♩=73) and work your way up, one bpm at a time, then back down.
- Always memorize the rhythms as fast as you can, so you can play them without reading them.
- Play each rhythm two times each, one leading into the next. Then jump around the page—for example, play two bars of B into two bars of D. Follow the same procedure, playing the rhythms as four-bar and eight-bar phrases.
- After a while, turn off the metronome, and play the rhythms with your internal clock. Always count yourself in before starting, and play with dynamics.

When you swing the sixteenth notes, the eighth notes will feel like quarter notes walking a bass line. Stay loose and relaxed, and make the triplets swing.

Listen to CD Track 9 to hear the time feel, and follow along with Chart 5, "Hip-Hop Shuffle," at the end of this chapter. Then start working on the following grooves, fills, and phrases.

Grooves

These one-bar grooves will work in the Intro/Section A of our tune. Push and swing the hi-hat with your right hand if you're right-handed, or with your left hand if you're left-handed. Swing these grooves hard, and play with dynamics. You know the routine by now.

Reminder: The accents above the backbeat on 2 and 4 are for the snare only. Do not accent the hi-hat.

The following two-bar grooves work with Section B. These are orchestrated on the ride cymbal, but you can also play them on hi-hat. Use the same procedure that you used with the Section A grooves. Follow the metronome markings, and increase your speed up or down one bpm at a time. This will also make you comfortable with the grooves at many different tempos.

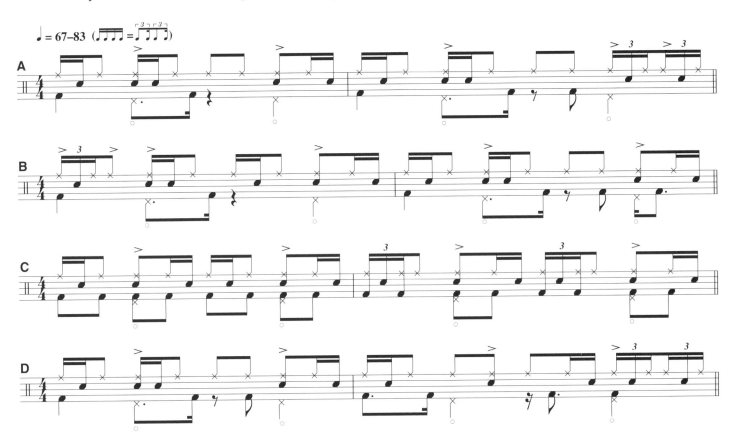

Worksheet

As you're working on the grooves and fills in this chapter, be sure to create some of your own on this worksheet.

Fills & Phrasing

It's time to play some fills with the hip-hop shuffle feel. First play each fill over and over again until you're comfortable with it. (Another approach is to play just the rhythm first on the snare drum against a quarter-note bass drum. This will get you acclimated to the rhythm before you work out the orchestration.) The next step is to play any of the grooves up to the fill, and then play the fill. Try three bars of groove into one bar of fill. This will give you a four-bar phrase. Other phrase combinations are:

2 bars of time + 2 bars of fill

4 bars of time + 4 bars of fill

6 bars of time + 2 bars of fill

8 bars of time + 4 bars of fill

Mix it up, and come up with some of your own combinations. Remember to make the fill come from the time feel of the groove. Let's begin.

Before we play Chart 5, let's check out the ensemble figure that appears at the end of the first Section B. It's a two-bar phrase.

Here's a four-bar phrase with the ensemble figure in the third and fourth bars. Repeat it over and over until it grooves at different tempos. When you get it together, work out some of your own phrases. Experiment with different rhythmic combinations to set up the figures.

CHART 5
Hip-Hop Shuffle

TRACK 9
with drums

TRACK 10
without drums

Time to put it all together. Use the grooves, fills, and phrases in the text to play the chart. Then play your own.

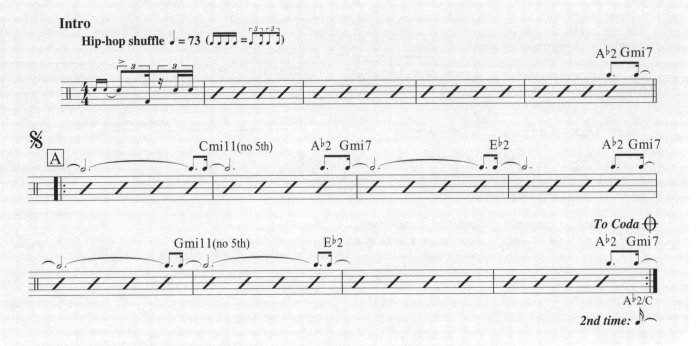

Intro	4 bars
A1	8 bars
A2	8 bars
B1	8 bars
A3	8 bars
A4	8 bars
Break	4 bars
B2	12 bars

Chapter Six
6 STRAIGHT TIME

In this chapter, the groove has more of straight time feel. The basic idea is to bounce and push all the eighth notes on the hi-hat or ride to create that forward motion. There's also strong eighth- and sixteenth-note syncopation between the bass and bass drum.

Listen to CD Track 11 to hear the time feel, and follow along with Chart 6, CD Track 11 "Moderate Funk," at the end of the chapter. Then start working on the following grooves, fills, and phrases.

Grooves

These one-bar grooves will work in Section A. Set your metronome or drum machine to ♩=112 and go for it. After you're comfortable playing each individual groove at different tempos, experiment with different phrasing combinations. You should know the routine by now.

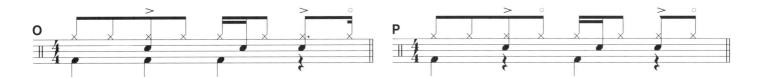

In the A sections and Introludes of the song, the bass line is the same or quite similar. The following are two four-bar grooves that you can play on the Introlude sections. Use the same procedure with these grooves. Remember to work on your phrasing and to increase the phrase length. Two-, four-, and eight-bar phrases are good lengths to begin with.

Worksheet

Write some of your own four-bar phrases on this worksheet. Try to keep an organized library of your rhythms, grooves, fills, and phrases.

Shifting the Hi-Hat

In previous chapters, we played fills at this point; however, I think you have enough fill ideas from past chapters. Let's talk instead about shifting the hi-hat. As a rule, we've kept the hi-hat or ride cymbal pretty steady thus far—steady eighths with some broken sixteenths. Let's check out some alternate hi-hat ideas that can be used on any of the grooves that we've played so far.

Try the following hi-hat "chicks and splashes" and alternate hi-hat/ride ideas. First work on them by themselves, then play them together—hi-hat chicks with alternate ideas on hi-hat or ride. Then try working them into your grooves, together or separately.

Hi-hat chicks and splashes

Alternate hi-hat/ride ideas

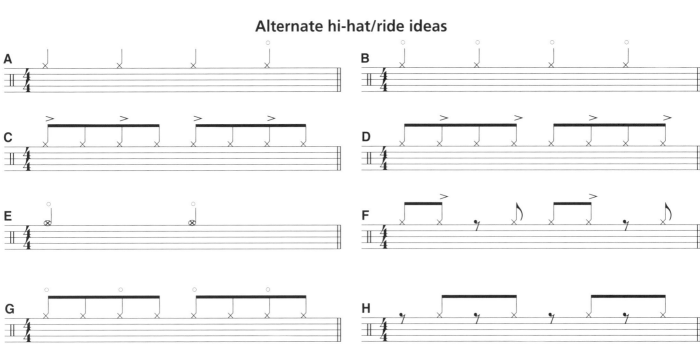

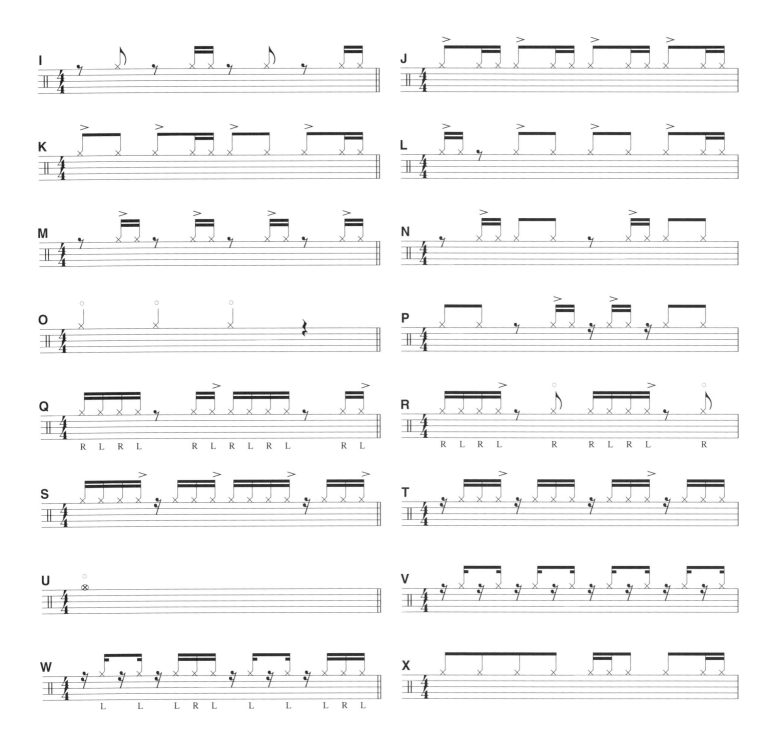

NOTE: The drums on this chapter's song, "Moderate Funk," were taken from a drum loop, and then the cymbal crashes and tom fills were overdubbed. This is a common way to work in today's world, with all the new technical approaches. It's good to spend some time thinking of the drumset as an overdub instrument. Just play tom fills or a ride cymbal or crashes. Work on it, and you will get comfortable with overdubbing individual parts of the kit.

Before we play the song, let's check out the ensemble figure that appears at the end of Section A. It's a two-bar phrase.

The following four-bar phrase features the ensemble figure in the third and fourth bars. Repeat it over and over until it grooves at the chart tempo (♩=112). Then work on it at different tempos. After you get it together, work out some of your own phrases. Experiment with different rhythmic combinations to set up the figures.

CHART 6
Moderate Funk

TRACK 11
with drums

TRACK 12
without drums

Time to play. Play the grooves and phrases in the text first. Also try out the various hi-hat/ride ideas. Then play your own ideas. You know the routine.

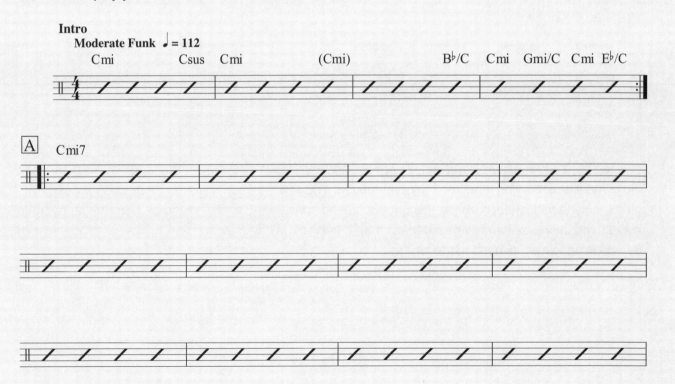

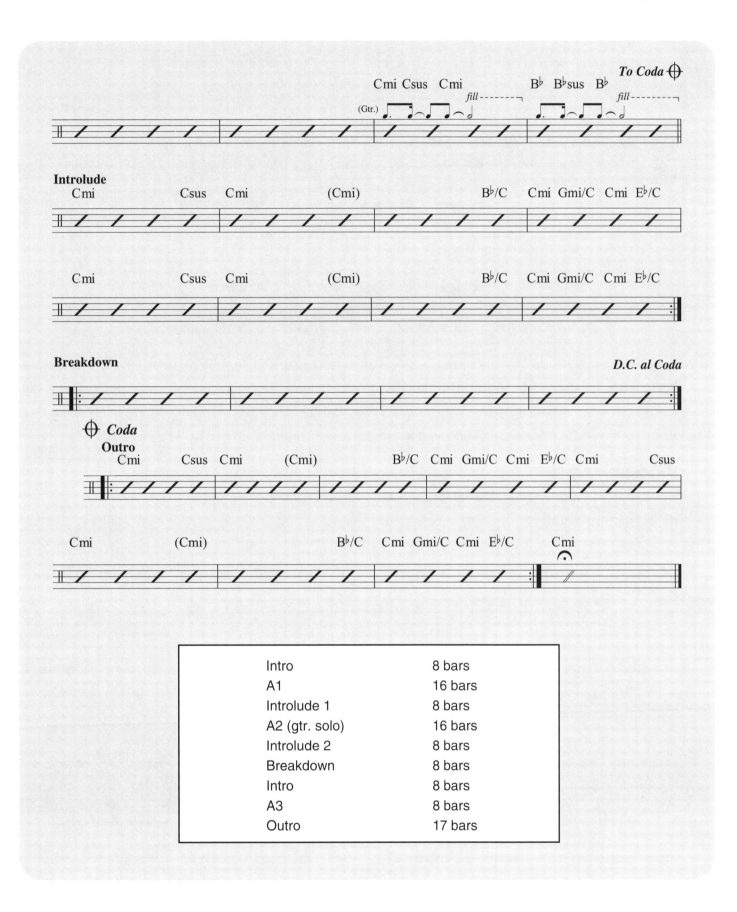

Intro	8 bars
A1	16 bars
Introlude 1	8 bars
A2 (gtr. solo)	16 bars
Introlude 2	8 bars
Breakdown	8 bars
Intro	8 bars
A3	8 bars
Outro	17 bars

Chapter Seven

7

MOVING THE SIXTEENTHS

In this final chapter, we'll play steady sixteenth notes on the hi-hat or ride cymbal with one hand. This is a straight time feel. The accent lope in the hi-hat will be in quarter notes or eighths, like this:

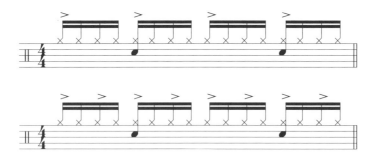

Accenting the sixteenths like this creates a sense of forward motion in the time feel; this is what I mean by "moving" the sixteenths. The feel is a funk R&B medium ballad.

Listen to CD Track 13 to hear the time feel, and follow along with Chart 7, CD Track 13 "R&B Funk," at the end of this chapter. Then start working on the following grooves, fills, and phrases.

Grooves

Let's begin with one-bar grooves. These will work in the Intro and Section A. By now you know the routine, so let's proceed.

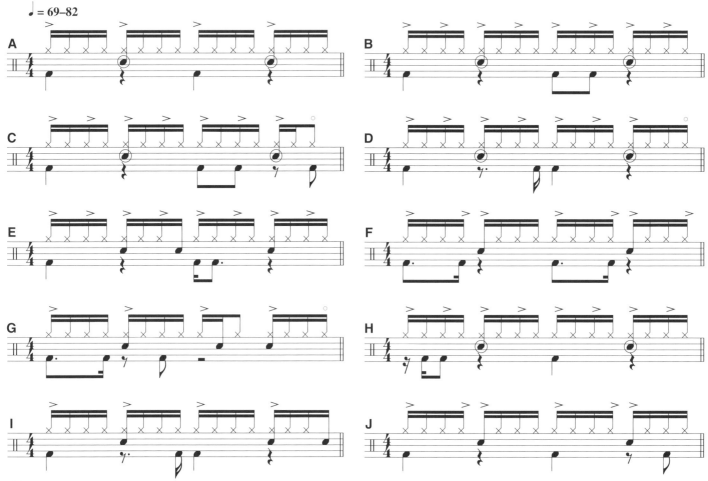

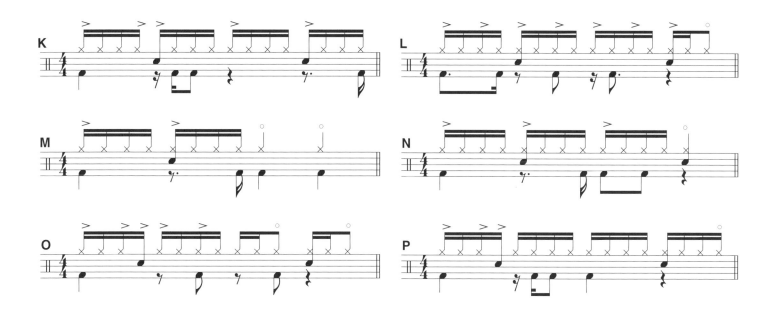

The following two-bar grooves work in the B Section. Notice the 32nd note ghosted snare drum in the first two. Experiment with different accents on the ride cymbal. You know the procedure, so go for it.

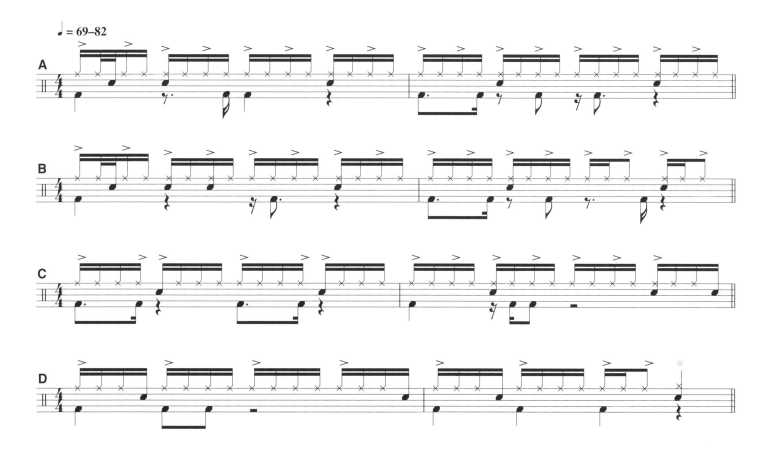

Worksheet

After you've worked on these grooves, write some of your own on this worksheet.

Shifting the Bass Drum

Use the following alternate bass drum ideas with any of the previous grooves in any of the chapters. These downbeats and syncopations will help you identify some hand and foot syncopations that might be uncomfortable for you to play at first—as you work on them, they will fall into place. Take your time and play within the metronome markings of the groove, and then experiment with other tempos.

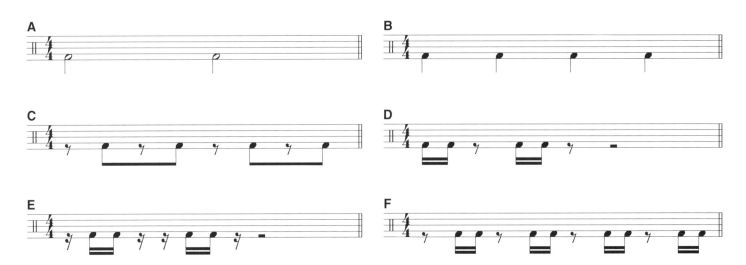

Before we play the chart, let's check out the ensemble figure that appears at the end of Section A going into Section B. This time the drumset orchestration is not written out. Experiment with your own ideas. Keep it simple at first. This example is a four-bar phrase—two bars of groove and two bars of the ensemble figure.

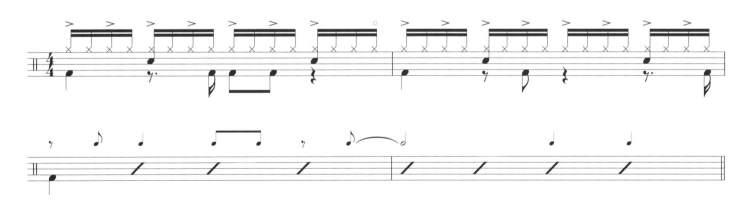

CHART 7
R&B Funk

TRACK 13 with drums   TRACK 14 without drums

Time to play. Remember: This is a medium tempo ballad, so lay back on your time feel.

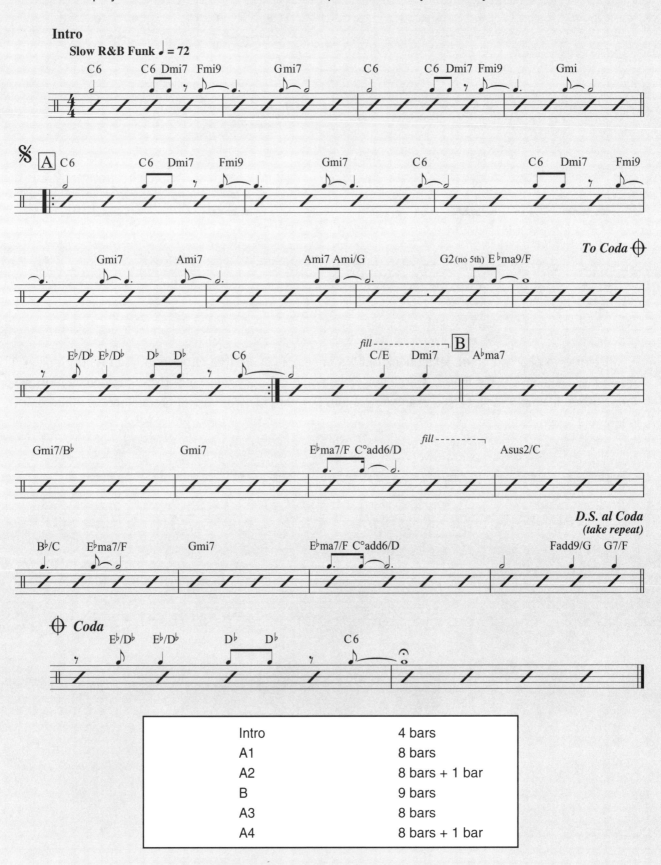

Intro	4 bars
A1	8 bars
A2	8 bars + 1 bar
B	9 bars
A3	8 bars
A4	8 bars + 1 bar